Pete Oldham

Kriminell gut lesen ENGLISCH

Fesselnde Kurzkrimis zur Förderung der Lesekompetenz

5.–7. Klasse

Auer Verlag

Gedruckt auf umweltbewusst gefertigtem, chlorfrei gebleichtem
und alterungsbeständigem Papier.

1. Auflage 2014
Nach den seit 2006 amtlich gültigen Regelungen der Rechtschreibung

Illustrationen: Stefanie Aufmuth, Julia Flasche, Steffen Jähde, Thorsten Trantow, Bettina Weyland
Umschlagfoto: panthermedia
Satz: Fotosatz H. Buck, Kumhausen
Druck und Bindung: Kessler Druck + Medien GmbH, Bobingen
ISBN 978-3-403-**07251**-5

www.auer-verlag.de

Inhalt

Vorwort

Die Geschichten und Übungen in diesem Heft sollen durch Spannung und interessante Inhalte den Wortschatz der Schülerinnen und Schüler erweitern, sie in die Textarbeit einführen und mit hilfreichen Lesetechniken bekannt machen. Das Hauptziel jedoch soll die Erkenntnis von jungen Menschen sein, dass Lesen Spaß machen kann. Bei einigen der Geschichten können die Schülerinnen und Schüler den Ermittlungen folgen, um durch logisches Denken dem Täter auf die Spur zu kommen. Bei anderen Geschichten lernen sie die humorvollen oder sogar die skurrilen Seite von Verbrechen kennen. Einige Texte bieten sich zudem als Sketche bzw. Rollenspiele an, sodass sich die Schülerinnen und Schüler aktiv und dramaturgisch beteiligen können.

Die Geschichten sprechen einerseits Schülerinnen wie Schüler an; anderseits sind sie in Bezug auf die Textlänge und den Schwierigkeitsgrad an die Lernstufen der Lernenden angepasst. Die Fähigkeit, mit unbekanntem Wortschatz umzugehen, ist deshalb ein primäres Lernziel. Das inhaltliche Verstehen der Texte wird durch eine reichliche Auswahl an Übungen und Aufgaben nach jedem Text unterstützt.
Bei einzelnen Geschichten bietet eine kurze Grammatikerklärung (grammar overview) eine zusätzliche Verständnishilfe.

Mit diesen Geschichten und Sachtexten möchte ich Ihnen und Ihren Schülerinnen und Schülern eine unterhaltsame Möglichkeit bieten, die Lesekompetenz zu fördern.

Ich wünsche viel Spaß bei der Arbeit!

Pete Oldham

An expensive trap

A police officer stops an expensive sports car at a radar trap *(Radarfalle)*. The driver is very angry. He jumps out of the car and throws a small plastic box onto the ground. Then he kicks it and jumps on it until it breaks into small pieces.

"Damn! Damn! Damn!" he swears. "I paid 750 dollars for that radar detector and it doesn't work!"

"Well, I don't know about that, sir," a police officer tells him. "I haven't got the radar today because I'm checking tyres."

Grammar overview

Simple Present
Hier wird eine Geschichte im Präsens erzählt. Beachte die folgenden Merkmale:

1. Bei der 3. Person Singular (he, she, it) wird ein 's' an die Grundform des Verbs angehängt:
Zeile 1: A police officer stop**s** a sports car.
Zeile 2: He (the driver) jump**s** out of the car and throw**s** …
Zeile 3: He kick**s** it until it break**s** into small pieces.
Zeile 4: He swear**s**.

2. Eine verneinte Aussage folgt dem Muster: do/does + not + Infinitivform:
Zeile 5: It **doesn't work**!
Zeile 6: I **don't know** about that.

3. Weitere Verben im Simple Present:
Zeile 1–2: The driver **is** very angry. (be: am, is, are)
Zeile 6–7: I **haven't got** the radar. (has got/hasn't got; have got/haven't got)

Weitere Verben/Zeitformen im Text
1. Simple Past: Die regelmäßigen Vergangenheitsformen sind leicht zu merken:
stop – stopp**ed**, jump – jump**ed**, walk – walk**ed**, play – play**ed**, kick – kick**ed**, …

Achtung: Die unregelmäßigen Formen müssen gelernt werden,
Beispiel: Zeile 4: I **paid** 750 dollars …

2. Present Progressive: Der Polizist benutzt hier das Present Progressive, weil er beschreibt, was er gerade macht:
Zeile 7: I**'m checking** tyres.

1. Translation in context: Find these words in the text. Think about the other words in the sentence and then guess *(erraten)* what they mean in German. Then check your results with a partner or look the words up in an English-German dictionary.

1. (line 3) ground ....
2. (line 3) until ....
3. (line 3) break ....
4. (line 3) pieces ....
5. (line 4) Damn! ....
6. (line 4) swear ....
7. (line 4) paid ....
8. (line 4) radar detector ....
9. (line 5) work ....
10. (line 7) tyres ....

2. Label the car with the words in the box below. You can use a dictionary.

bag   brake light   bumper   hubcap   plastic box
roof rack   suitcase   tyre   window

1. ....
2. ....
3. ....
4. ....
5. ....
6. ....
7. ....
8. ....
9. ....

Three liars: A sketch

① Mr Tate: *[Comes in the front door.]* Hello, Jane. Look what I've got.

② Mrs Tate: Hello, dear. Is that a new house robot, Dave?

③ Mr Tate: Yes, I bought it on my way home.

④ Mrs Tate: Why? We've got enough house robots, Dave. We don't need another.

⑤ Mr Tate: This robot can tell if someone is telling the truth *(Wahrheit)* or lying *(lügen)*. It can be useful when salesmen *(Verkäufer)* try to sell us something.

⑥ Mrs Tate: How does it work?

⑦ Mr Tate: I can show you. Let's try it out on our son. Where is he?

⑧ Mrs Tate: He's upstairs in his room.

⑨ Mr Tate: Rod! Rod!

⑩ Rod Tate: What is it now?

⑪ Mr Tate: Come down here, Rod. This is a new robot and it can tell when people are lying. I want to ask you something.

⑫ Rod Tate: *[Comes down the stairs.]* What?

⑬ Mr Tate: Where were you this morning?

⑭ Rod Tate: I was at school, of course.
[The robot buzzes (surrt).]
OK, OK. I was at a friend's house. We did our homework together.
[The robot buzzes.]
OK! There was a party. But I only drank orange juice.
[The robot buzzes.]
OK! I had a glass of whisky – but only one!
[The robot buzzes.]
OK, OK. I had two glasses of whisky and a rum and coke. That's the truth!

⑮ Mr Tate: That's disgraceful *(beschämend)*! At your age I didn't even know what alcohol was!
[The robot buzzes.]

⑯ Mrs Tate: Ha ha! You lied too, Dave. After all, Rod is your son.
[The robot buzzes.]

Grammar overview

Verben im Simple Present

have got

Zeile 2: Look what **I've got**.
Aussagen: has got/hasn't got, have got/haven't got
Frage: Has he got …?/Have you got …?

be

Zeile 3: **Is** that a new house robot, Dave?
Aussagen: am/am not, is/isn't, are/aren't
Frage: Am I …?/Is it …?/Are we …?

need (s. auch alle anderen Vollverben, z. B. come, tell, buy, sell, …)

Zeile 5: We **don't need** another.
Aussagen: needs/doesn't need, need/don't need
Frage: Do I need a …?/Does she need a …?

Modale Hilfsverben im Simple Present

Zeile 6: This robot **can tell** if someone is telling the truth or lying.
Zeile 6–7: It **can be** useful when salesmen try to sell us something.

Verben im Present Progressive

Zeile 6: This robot can tell if someone **is telling** the truth or **lying**.
Zeile 13–14: It can tell when people **are lying**.

Verben im Simple Past

Verben	*Beispielsätze*
be: was/wasn't, were/weren't	Was she OK?/Were you there?
buy: bought/didn't buy	Did they buy a new car?
do: did/didn't	Did he do his homework?
drink: drank/didn't drink	Did Rod drink alcohol?
have: had/didn't have	Did they have a good time?
lie: lied/didn't lie	Did you lie to me?
know: knew/didn't know	Did they know about it?

1. Complete the sentences with the correct simple present forms of the verbs in brackets.

1. (have got) Mr Tate ………………… something.
2. (be – not be) It ………………… a new robot and Mrs Tate ………………… pleased.
3. (think) She ………………… they have enough house robots.
4. (not want) She ………………… another robot.
5. (show) Mr Tate ………………… her what the new robot can do.
6. (test – ask) He ………………… the robot on his son and ………………… him a question.
7. (lie – buzz) His son ………………… to him and the robot ………………… .

2. Are these statements true (T), false (F) or not in the text (N)?

1. Dave Tate bought the new house robot. ....
2. He bought it at a local supermarket. ....
3. Mrs Tate thinks the new robot is useful. ....
4. Mr Tate tests the robot on his son. ....
5. The Tates also have a daughter. ....
6. Rod Tate is a pupil at a local school. ....
7. Rod Tate tells his parents two lies. ....
8. Dave Tate is Mrs Tate's second husband. ....

3. Work with three partners, read the dialogue and write four role cards. Then act out the dialogue. Afterwards swap roles and act out the dialogue again.

Dave Tate

① *[Comes in the front door.]* Hello, Jane. Look what I've got.

③ Yes, I bought it on my way home.

⑤ …

etc.

Jane Tate

② Hello, dear. Is that a new house robot, Dave?

④ Why? …

⑥ How …?

etc.

Rod Tate

⑩ What is it now?

⑫ *[Comes down the stairs.]* What?

⑭ I was …

etc.

Robot

buzzes (x 6)

4. What do you think these words might mean in German? Don't use a dictionary. Then compare with a partner.

a) **'House' words**

1. housecat ....
2. house husband ....
3. housewife ....
4. household ....
5. housework ....
6. housekeeper ....
7. householder ....
8. housebreaker ....

b) **'Home' words**

1. homework ....
2. homeless ....
3. home-made ....
4. homeowner ....
5. homesick ....
6. home town ....
7. homeworker ....
8. homeland ....

5. Translate these sentences into German.

1. My mother works at home. She's a homeworker.

....

2. My computer doesn't work. I think it's broken.

....

A serial killer

Detective Inspector Diana Woodford looks at the team of detectives in front of her. "We've got three crime scenes *(Tatorte)* and three bodies *(Leichen)*." She turns around and points to a photo on the wall behind her. "On Monday morning we get a letter. A man reports a murder *(Mord)* and gives us an address. It's a flat in the city centre. When we get there, we find a man in the kitchen with his head in a bowl of muesli. He's dead and the crime lab *(Kriminallabor)* finds poison *(Gift)* in his breakfast muesli."

D. I. Woodford points to another photo. "On Tuesday we get another letter. It tells us about another murder at a different address. This time it's a warehouse *(Lagerhalle)* near the docks *(Hafenanlagen)*. Inside we find the body of a man under a very heavy pallet of honey smacks®. He's very dead."

D. I. Woodford points to a third photo. "This morning we get another letter with the address of a big house near the park. There we find a dead woman in a bath of milk and cornflakes."

One of her team holds up a newspaper. "The local press already have the story, Ma'am. And they have a name for the killer, too."

THE BIGGLESBY HEROLD

POLICE LOOK FOR A CEREAL KILLER

Grammar overview

Simple Present

1. Bei einer Geschichte oder Erzählung beschreibt das Simple Present Ereignisse, die gerade geschehen.
Zeile 1: Detective Inspector Diana Woodford **looks** at the team of detectives in front of her.
Zeile 2: We'**ve got** three crime scenes and three bodies.
Zeile 2–3: She **turns** around and **points** to a photo on the wall behind her.

2. Das Simple Present kann auch bei einer Beschreibung von Ereignissen in einer zeitlichen Abfolge (wie z. B. bei einem Fahrplan oder Ablaufplan) verwendet werden – auch wenn diese Ereignisse in der Vergangenheit geschahen.
Zeile 3: On Monday morning we **get** a letter.
Zeile 4: A man **reports** a murder and **gives** us an address.

1. Fill in the missing words.

1. When he turns ...., he can see us.
2. Sarah, can you point .... your drawing, please?
3. I don't like the way my teacher looks .... me!
4. That's a wonderful drawing, Jane. Please hold it ....
5. Sally! What have you .... behind your back?

2. Complete the sentences below with words from the text.

D. I. Woodford and her team are looking for a .... (1) killer. The killer reports the .... (2) to the police and gives them the .... (3). The three crimes all happen in the .... (4) and have something to do with breakfast .... (5). For the first crime the killer uses .... (6). For the second crime he uses a .... (7) of honey smacks® and for the third crime he kills a woman in a .... (8) of .... (9) and cornflakes. This is why the newspaper calls him a ".............................. (10) killer".

3. Read the following e-mails and think about the information in them. How can this information help to find the killer? Write your answer in your exercise book.

TO:	D. I. Woodford
COPY:	
SUBJECT:	LAB RESULTS
FROM:	info@bigg_crimelab.uk

Dear Detective Inspector Woodford,

We've got a long brown hair from crime scene #3 and another long brown hair from letter #2. Both hairs are from a dog.
Do you want us to do a DNA test and identify the type of dog?

Best wishes
Dr. C. Reed

TO:	D. I. Woodford
COPY:	
SUBJECT:	POSTBOX COLLECTIONS
FROM:	dcsimpson@cid_bigg.uk

Dear Detective Inspector Woodford,

There are 27 postboxes in Bigglesby. I've marked them on a map (see enclosure).
A postman collects the letters from the postboxes and takes them to the main post office at these times: 9:30 a.m., 12:30 p.m. and 4:15 p.m.

Best wishes
D. C. Simpson

4. Reconstruct this discussion between D. I. Woodford and her crime team.

D. I. Woodford: We've got some good news from the crime lab. The killer has got a dog with long brown hair. Has anyone got any ideas?

1: …

D. I. Woodford: Yes, Alan, but there are lots of people with dogs in Bigglesby, so there will be lots of people on the list.

2: …

D. I. Woodford: Thanks, Susan. So we can make a list of just the people with long-haired, brown dogs. That will be much smaller. OK, Alan. That's your job.

3: …

D. I. Woodford: Good. Fax the list as soon as you can, Alan. It's now 2 p.m. We need your list before the last post at 4:15 p.m.

4: …

D. I. Woodford: Yes, I know, Susan. But there's a good chance that the killer will send the letter with the last post at 4:15 p.m. I've got a job for you, too.

5: …

D. I. Woodford: I want you to go to the traffic control room. Here is a map of all postboxes in Bigglesby. Find out how many of them we can watch on surveillance cameras *(Überwachungskameras)*. Send me a list of postboxes where there are no cameras.

E
Detective Constable Alan Taylor:
People with dogs must have a dog licence. We can make a list.

B
Detective Constable Alan Taylor:
Thanks, Ma'am. I'll go straight to the town hall now.

A
Detective Constable Susan Simpson:
Good. What do you want me to do, Ma'am?

C
Detective Constable Susan Simpson:
Perhaps we are already too late!

D
Detective Constable Susan Simpson:
The dog licences have a description of the dog, Ma'am.

1 ...., 2 ...., 3 ...., 4 ...., 5 ....

5. Work with two partners. Take over the three roles and act out the dialogues.

6. The crime team catch the cereal killer. It's a man called Max Gregory. Write a newspaper article about it in your exercise book.

Two swindlers

Tony sees his sister Sabrina in the school playground. She's with her friend Carmen Davies.

"Hi, sis. I need 15 pounds, but I've only got ten pounds. Can you lend me five pounds?"

"Hi, Tony. No, I'm sorry. I haven't got any pocket money left. But Carmen has got ten pounds! Isn't that right, Carmen?"

"Yes, I've got ten pounds, but I need the money. I want to buy a mobile phone card for 15 pounds."

Tony thinks and then he makes Carmen an offer.

"Look, we both need 15 pounds. Let's have a quiz about animals. If I can't answer your question, you get my ten pounds. And if you can't answer my question, I get your ten pounds. OK?"

Carmen thinks about it.

"Don't do it, Carmen," Sabrina warns her. "Tony is a swindler. He knows lots about animals. It's his favourite subject. He can't lose."

Carmen thinks carefully.

"Well, he thinks he can't lose. OK, Tony. But because you know more about animals than I do, it's only fair that if I can't answer your question, I only give you five pounds. Do you agree?"

Tony thinks about it. He's sure he can't lose.

"OK, I agree. If I don't know the answer to your question, I give you ten pounds. If you don't know the answer to my question, you give me five pounds. You can also ask the first question."

"Thanks, Tony. That's very fair. OK, here's my question: What animal is red, white and blue, is 80 centimetres long and has four wings, 14 legs and three eyes?"

Tony thinks about it for a minute, then he gives up.

"I don't know. OK. Here are my ten pounds. What's the answer?"

Carmen smiles.

"I don't know either. Here are my five pounds."

Sabrina laughs.

"That serves you right, Tony! Girls are better swindlers!"

1. Translation in context: Find the English translations in the text of these German words.

1. Schulhof ....
2. leihen ....
3. Taschengeld ....
4. Handy ....
5. Angebot ....
6. denken ....
7. Schwindler ....
8. Lieblingsthema ....
9. verlieren ....
10. zustimmen ....

2. Translate these phrases into German.

1. I don't know either. ....

2. That serves you right. ....

3. Answer these questions about the text.

1. What does Carmen Davies want to buy?

....

2. How much money does Carmen need?

....

3. What do Carmen and Tony agree to do?

....

4. Why does Tony think he can't lose?

....

5. How does Carmen win the money?

....

4. Read Carmen's question and draw the animal she describes.

Case 273, part 1

Detective Inspector Ben Callahan is reading the documents in case file *(Fallakte)* 273. He's writing a timeline on his laptop.

9:23 a.m.	Mrs J. Evans, a neighbour, calls the local police station and reports a bad smell in flat number 26.
9:52 a.m.	Police Officer Riley and Police Officer Greenwood arrive at flat 26. The door is locked and the neighbours don't have a key. The police officers call a key service.
10:22 a.m.	A woman arrives from the key service and opens the door of the flat. It belongs to *(gehört)* a Mr F. Forster.
10:25 a.m.	The police officers find a body *(Leiche)* in the bedroom. They call the forensic *(gerichtsmedizinisches)* team and wait outside the flat.
10:48 a.m.	The forensic team (two crime-scene *(Tatort)* specialists and a doctor) arrive. They examine *(untersuchen)* the body and the flat.
11:19 a.m.	The forensic team write their report. The main points are: – The smell in the bedroom was very bad. The doctor needed a breathing mask. – The body was a very fat man (390 pounds weight). – Time of death was between midnight and 1 a.m. – There were no wounds *(Wunden)* on the body. – All the windows in the flat were closed and locked. – Dirty plates and empty tins and bottles were in the kitchen. The man's last meal was enormous. He ate six tins of baked beans *(gebackene Bohnen)* with four slices *(Scheiben)* of toast with Gorgonzola cheese and he drank six bottles of beer.

1. Look at the pictures below. Find the English names for these things in the text.

1. 

....

2. 

....

3. 

....

4. 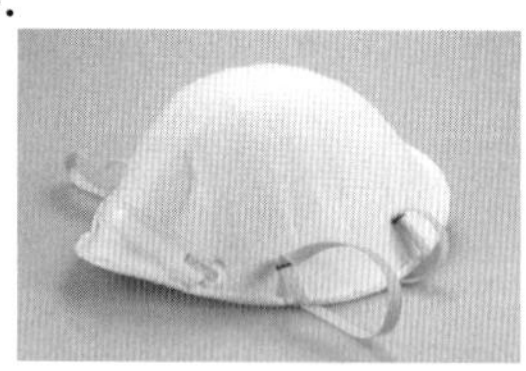

....

5. 

....

6. 

....

7. 

....

8. 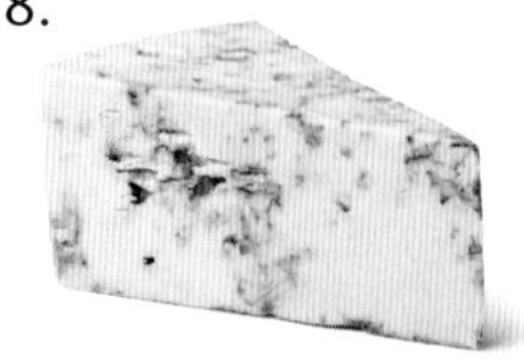

....

2. Complete each sentence with an English word from the text. Then fill in the crossword with the German translations (ü = ue etc.).

Across

5. There were also six empty .... of beer.

7. Mrs Evans calls the local ....

9. The .... in the bedroom was closed and locked.

11. Mrs J. Evans is a .... of Mr Forster.

15. There were no .... on the body.

17. The police officers call a ....

18. Mr Forster liked .... and Gorgonzola cheese!

19. Mr Forster died between .... and one o'clock in the morning.

20. D.I. Callahan is reading a case ....

Down

1. Nobody has a .... to flat 26.

2. Mr Forster's .... is in the bedroom.

3. There was a dirty .... in the kitchen with some beans on it.

4. The doctor needed a ....

6. He also ate four .... of toast.

8. Two specialists examine the ....

10. A doctor examines the body in the ....

12. Mr Forster's last .... was baked beans.

13. There were six empty .... of baked beans.

14. Mrs Evans reports a .... from the flat.

15. The .... belongs to a Mr F. Forster.

16. The doctor calculated *(berechnete)* the time of ....

3. What is the metric weight *(Gewicht)* of the dead man?
(1 pound = 0.4536 kilogramme)

The dead man weighs .... kg.

4. Mr Forster wasn't murdered *(ermordet)*. What facts support this statement?

....

....

....

....

5. What do you think killed Mr Forster? Make a list of the things you think are suspicious *(verdächtig)*.

....

....

....

Case 273, part 2

Doctor Samantha Neville, the forensic doctor, calls Detective Inspector Callahan.

Sam: Hi, Ben. I've got the autopsy results for Mr Forster. I know how he died.

Ben: Let me guess. I think his last meal killed him. He ate and drank too much and he had a heart attack and died in his sleep.

Sam: Well, he ate and drank too much, but he didn't die of a heart attack. He was killed by a mixture of methane and carbon dioxide. It's a lethal poison gas!

Ben: Was that the cause of the terrible smell?

Sam: Yes, that's right.

Ben: So he was murdered!

Sam: No. We all produce methane and carbon dioxide when we digest our meals. It's a natural product.

Ben: But we don't all die in our sleep!

Sam: No, but we don't weigh almost 177 kilos, we don't all sleep with the window closed and we certainly don't eat six tins of baked beans with Gorgonzola cheese and drink six bottles of beer before we go to bed!

Ben: What do I put in my report, Sam? I can't write: "Mr Forster died from poisonous farts *(giftige Furze)*!"

Sam: Just write: "Mr Forster died of natural causes. See autopsy report."

Ben: Thanks, Sam. I'll do that.

6. Look at the following words from the text in context. What do they mean in German? Check your answers with an English-German dictionary.

1. autopsy ....
2. results ....
3. guess ....
4. heart attack ....
5. methane ....
6. carbon dioxide (CO_2) ....
7. lethal ....
8. poison gas ....
9. produce ....
10. digest ....

Multitasking

The following question comes from an examination paper for police officers in the Canadian Metropolitan Police:

You're walking across a bridge over a river when just in front of you a car runs into the back of a bus. The driver and a woman passenger are injured *(verletzt)*. There is a strong smell of alcohol and empty vodka bottles on the back seat. The man has no driving licence or car insurance *(Versicherung)* and you know the woman – it's the wife of an important government *(Regierung)* minister. Just then a car stops and the driver offers *(bietet an)* his help. You recognize him – he's a mad killer who has just escaped *(geflüchtet)* from an asylum *(Irrenanstalt)*. A man jumps out of the bus and shouts for help. His wife is having a baby *(bekommt ein Kind)*. The driver of the bus was thrown into the river and now she's screaming *(schreit)* for help because she can't swim. Describe what you would do.

The question was a test in multitasking: Make a list of priorities *(Rangordnung)* and deal with each problem in that order. However, it was too difficult for the candidates and only one answered it. He wrote just one sentence: Take off uniform and mix with the crowd.

Grammar overview

Zeitformen im Text

1. Simple Present: Es wird ein unveränderbarer Zustand beschrieben:
Zeile 1: This question **comes from** a police exam.

2. Present Progressive: Zuerst wird die Tätigkeit beschrieben, die zur Zeit der anderen Ereignisse noch im Gange war. Was danach geschieht, wird im Simple present beschrieben:
Zeile 3–4: You'**re walking across** a bridge. A car **runs into** a bus.
The driver and a woman passenger are injured. (Übersetzung: Entweder als Adjektiv übersetzen (… sind verletzt) oder als Passivform (… werden verletzt).)

3. Present Perfect: Diese Zeitform beschreibt ein Geschehen, das in der Vergangenheit angefangen hat und noch in die Gegenwart wirkt.
Zeile 8–9: The mad killer **has** just **escaped** from an asylum.

4. Simple Past: Diese Zeitform beschreibt Handlungen in der Vergangenheit, die bereits abgeschlossen sind:
Zeile 11: The driver of the bus **was thrown** into the river. (Übersetzung: Als Passivform: … wurde in den Fluss geworfen)
Zeile 13–15: It **was** a test in multitasking, but only one candidate **answered** it.

1. What do the pictures show? Find the English words for these things in the text.

....

....

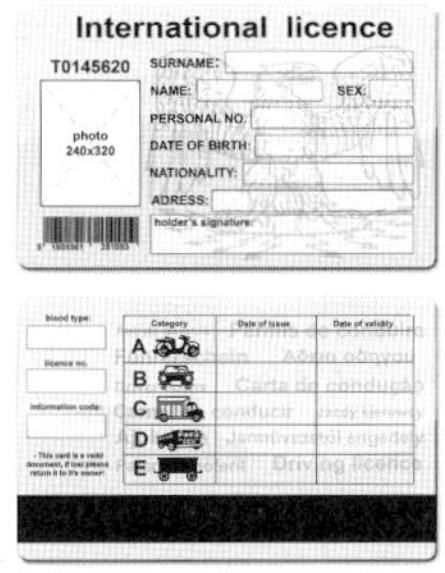

....

....

....

....

2. Read the multitasking question in the text and imagine you are a police officer in the exam and then make a priority list of problems below: from 1 (= the most important) to 9 (= the least important). Remember, there is no 'right' or 'wrong' answer.

Report the car/bus crash.

Priority number: ....

Call paramedics (Sanitäter)*: injured man and woman in car.*

Priority number: ....

Call paramedics: woman having baby.

Priority number: ....

Call government minister: wife injured.

Priority number: ....

Give driver of car a breathalyzer test (Alkoholtest).

Priority number: ....

Call for help/back up: mad killer.

Priority number: ....

Arrest driver of car: no licence or insurance.

Priority number: ....

Organize help for woman in river.

Priority number: ....

Call river police: woman in river.

Priority number: ....

3. Complete the following sentences with the correct prepositions.

My wife comes ………………………… (1) a small village in Cornwall. Last summer we stayed ………………………… (2) her parents there. We drove ………………………… (3) a very old stone bridge ………………………… (4) a small river. We parked the car ………………………… (5) the car park ………………………… (6) the end of the bridge and walked ………………………… (7) the village because the streets are too narrow ………………………… (8) cars.

4. Use an English-German dictionary and find the opposites of these words from the text.

Text	Opposite	German
1. in front of	…………………………	…………………………
2. strong	…………………………	…………………………
3. empty	…………………………	…………………………
4. back seat	…………………………	…………………………
5. important	…………………………	…………………………
6. mad	…………………………	…………………………
7. difficult	…………………………	…………………………
8. take off (clothes)	…………………………	…………………………

5. Complete the following sentences with information from the text.

1. The people in the car were both ………………………… in the crash.
2. The ………………………… of the car ………………………… a driving licence.
3. His passenger was the ………………………… .
4. The driver who stopped and offered help was a ………………………… .
5. A woman on the bus was ………………………… and her husband was shouting ………………………… .
6. The woman in the river was the ………………………… .

The cheeky shoplifter

Emily Mayfield's first day in her new job as a store detective was terrible! On the store camera she saw a young girl put an expensive blouse into her shopping bag. Emily followed the young girl around the store and saw her put three more blouses, two skirts and two cashmere sweaters into her shopping bag. Then the girl looked at some cosmetics and Emily saw mascara, lipsticks and nail varnish go into her shopping bag. Then the girl went into the ladies' toilet. Emily waited until the girl came out and watched her walk past the cash desk and out of the store. Emily ran outside and stopped the girl in the street. She took her back to the store and called the police. Ten minutes later a policewoman arrived. She searched *(durchsuchte)* the girl and looked inside her shopping bag. There were six cheap T-shirts in the bag. The young girl smiled and took a passport out of her coat pocket and gave it to the policewoman. "She's only twelve years old and here are receipts for the T-shirts," the policewoman told Emily. "I'm sorry, but I must let her go." The young girl smiled at Emily and the policewoman, took back her passport and her bag and coolly walked out of the store.

Six weeks later Emily saw the girl again. Emily followed her around the store and watched her steal clothes and cosmetics. Emily saw her go into the ladies' toilet again. This time she asked another store detective to help her. They saw the girl come out of the toilet about ten minutes later and Emily followed her out into the street. Emily stopped her again and brought her back to the store and called the police. The same policewoman arrived and she recognized the girl. "Oh, not you again!" When she searched the girl and her shopping bags, it was the same as last time; the girl wasn't wearing or carrying the stolen things. The young girl gave the policewoman her passport again and smiled at her and Emily. Emily smiled back and looked at her watch. "Let's just wait a minute or so." Just then the other store detective came. He was holding a fat woman in a long coat. She was shouting and struggling *(wehrte sich)*. When the policewoman searched her, they discovered that the woman wasn't really fat. Under her long coat she was wearing five blouses, two sweaters, a leather jacket, four skirts and a bag full of cosmetics!

1. What are the English words for the things in the photos?

1.

2.

3.

4.

5.
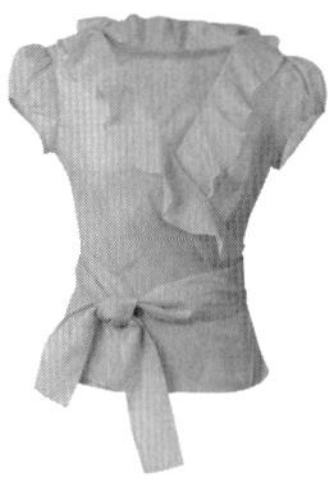

6.

7.

8.

9.

10.

2. Complete the sentences with the words from the box.

cash desk	cheap	cosmetics	expensive	fat	ladies' toilet
leather	receipts	steal	stolen		

1. A Rolex is a very .... watch.
2. Mascara, nail varnish and face cream are ....
3. The .... is on the second floor.
4. In a motorway self-service restaurant people must pay for their food at the ....
5. This T-shirt only costs six dollars. That's ....
6. When I buy clothes, I always keep the .... because I might want to take something back.
7. Shoplifters are people who .... things from shops and stores.
8. A policewoman searched the woman and found the .... cosmetics in a bag under her skirt.
9. Groucho Marx: An opera is never over until the .... lady sings!
10. I liked a .... handbag, but it was much too expensive.

3. Fill in the missing prepositions.

I walked .... (1) the store. I looked .... (2) some cosmetics. I chose a face cream and a perfume and took them .... (3) the cash desk. I checked the receipts and put them .... (4) my handbag. I tried .... (5) two blouses, but I didn't like them and put them .... (6). Then I looked .... (7) a leather jacket under 100 dollars.

4. Answer these questions about the text.

1. Why did Emily wait until the girl was in the street before she stopped her?

2. Why did Emily call a policewoman to search the girl?

3. Why did the policewoman let the girl go?

4. Why do you think that the girl didn't have the stolen clothes or cosmetics?

5. Where did the girl get the T-shirts and the receipts?

6. How did Emily catch the girl the second time?

5. Find the simple past verb forms of these verbs from the text.

1. be		7. watch	
2. see		8. run	
3. put		9. stop	
4. go		10. take	
5. wait		11. call	
6. come		12. arrive	

6. Look at the signs and answer the questions. You can use a dictionary.

Store A

Win a Free Ride
in a Police Car just by shoplifting from this store.

Lucky winners can also get their name in the newspaper for their family and friends to see!

Make Mom & Dad proud!

Store B

PLEASE HELP US BY STEALING ONLY THE STUFF WE CAN'T SELL. THANK YOU

Store C

SECURITY NOTICE

THIS AREA IS UNDER 24 HOUR TV SURVEILLANCE. SHOPLIFTERS WILL BE PROSECUTED.

Store D

Shoplifting is a Crime

If you steal, our cameras will catch you.

Store E

THIS STORE IS PATROLLED BY SECURITY PERSONNEL

Store F

SHOPLIFTERS WILL BE TERMINATED!

1. Which stores have TV cameras? ....
2. Which store has got detectives that walk around the store? ....
3. Which stores report shoplifters to the police? ....
4. Which store gives the names of shoplifters to a local newspaper? ....
5. Which store asks shoplifters to help them? ....
6. How? Explain in German. ....

   ....
7. What does Store F threaten *(droht)* to do to shoplifters? Explain in German. ....

   ....
8. Is this a serious threat or just a joke? Explain in German. ....

   ....

Two smugglers

At the harbour in Algeciras the Spanish customs officer looked at the passports of the two young backpackers. They had arrived on the evening ferry from Tangier in Morocco. "Anything to declare?" she asked. The young man and the young woman both shook their heads. "No, nothing." The customs officer decided to check them. "Please unpack your rucksacks." She looked through their clothes carefully. They had the usual things: shirts, blouses, socks, underwear, jeans etc. and they were all well-used. There were no drugs, alcohol or cigarettes. "Thank you. Enjoy your visit."

Two weeks later the same customs officer noticed the two backpackers again. She checked their passports. They had left Algeciras that morning on the ferry to Tangier in Morocco and now they were returning on the evening ferry. There and back in just one day? She asked them to unpack their rucksacks. She found only old clothes again. She let them go, but made a note of their names and told her colleagues about them. The following week another customs officer noticed them returning on the same ferry from Tangier. He also searched their rucksacks, but he couldn't find anything illegal. The young couple made the same round trip two or three times a month. They always left on the early morning ferry and returned on the evening ferry. Perhaps they were selling their old clothes? But they wouldn't make any money with old clothes and it wasn't illegal. All the customs officers thought they must be smuggling something more valuable than old clothes. The young couple and their backpacks were searched some more times, but nothing was ever found. It was a puzzle.

The puzzle was solved some weeks later when the customs officer from Algeciras and her husband went shopping in Malaga one Saturday morning. They were walking around the market in Malaga when the customs officer saw the two young backpackers. They had a small market stall. And then she saw what they were selling!

1. Some words in English and German are very similar. Find the English words with the same meaning in the text.

1. Hafen ....
2. Reisepass ....
3. Fähre ....
4. auspacken ....
5. Bluse ....
6. Leder ....
7. Drogen ....
8. Kollegen ....
9. Schmuggler ....
10. Markt ....

2. Words in context: Match the English words from the text with their translations in German.

1.	customs officer	A	den Kopf schütteln
2.	backpackers	B	verdächtig/suspekt
3.	valuable	C	Unterwäsche
4.	underwear	D	Notiz
5.	search	E	Rucksacktouristen
6.	shake one's head	F	Marktstand
7.	note	G	wertvoll
8.	couple	H	Zollbeamter
9.	suspicious	I	durchsuchen
10.	market stall	J	Pärchen/Paar

1. .... 2. .... 3. .... 4. .... 5. .... 6. .... 7. .... 8. .... 9. .... 10. ....

3. Translate these sentences into German.

1. Anything to declare? ....

2. Please unpack your rucksacks. ....

4. What were the young couple smuggling and selling on the market?

First make a list of everything they had. Then cross out *(streiche durch)* the things that weren't illegal. Whatever is left over must be what they were smuggling.

....

....

....

....

....

....

They were smuggling ....

5. Answer these questions about the text.

1. What did the two backpackers often do?

....

....

2. Why did the customs officers think that this was suspicious?

....

....

3. What did the customs officers usually find in the backpacks of the young couple?

....

6. Link the infinitive forms of the verbs from the text with their simple past forms.

couldn't

left

shake

see

had

be

told

made

can't

shook

tell

went

found

thought

find

think

leave

saw

make

was/were

have

go

7. Complete this list of verbs.

1.	haben	have	had
2.	schütteln	shake	shook
3.	sein	be	was/were
4.	finden	....	....
5.	lassen	....	....
6.	machen	....	....
7.	erzählen/berichten	....	....
8.	verlassen	....	....
9.	denken/meinen	....	....
10.	gehen	....	....
11.	sehen	....	....

8. Fill in the simple past passive forms of the verbs in brackets.

The passports of the two backpackers (1. check) ....

carefully and they (2. ask) .... to unpack their rucksacks.

Their names (3. note) .... and they (4. search)

.... some more times, but nothing illegal (5. find)

....

The puzzle (6. solve) .... some weeks later.

The young couple (7. see) .... in the market at Malaga.

9. You are going backpacking in Spain for a week. What things would you take? Use a German-English dictionary and make a list in German and a list in English.

The clever sausage thief

Harriet's best friend was her Labrador dog, Toby. He walked to school with her every day. Toby knew he wasn't allowed in the school, so they said goodbye at the school gates and Toby walked back home. In the afternoon Toby met Harriet at the school gates and they went home together. Harriet's English teacher was Mrs Collins. She had a collie and she invited Harriet and Toby to visit her dog training club that Saturday afternoon.

Harriet and Toby watched dogs and their owners walk around in circles *(Kreise)*, they watched dogs run across planks and jump over walls and fences. Toby wasn't very interested. Then a man from the club came out with a big basket of sausages. Toby's ears stood up when he smelled them. He loved sausages! Harriet's teacher explained that it was a contest *(Wettbewerb)* and any dog could take part *(teilnehmen)*. Harriet saw that Toby was interested and told Mrs Collins that they would take part. There were seven other dogs in the contest. The rules were very simple. The eight owners stood two metres in front of their dogs and a sausage was put between them. The game started when the judge *(Preisrichter)* blew a whistle. The owners had to wait until they heard him blow the whistle again and then they could tell their dogs that they could eat the sausage. The dogs had to wait until then. Harriet explained the rules to Toby. Her teacher was sceptical. "Dogs don't really understand what you are saying when you talk to them. If he has never done it before, he won't know what to do." The judge walked along the line of dogs and carefully placed a sausage in front of each dog. Toby and Harriet were at the end of the line. Toby was very excited. When the judge blew the whistle, he jumped up and ran along the line of dogs and gobbled down *(herunterschlingen)* each sausage as he passed. All the other dogs snarled! Then Toby ran back to Harriet and sat down again in front of his own sausage. The judge blew his whistle again and when Harriet shouted "Go, Toby!" he jumped forward and ate his own sausage. Then all the other dogs ran around Toby and barked angrily. Their owners ran around after them and shouted. It was chaos. Toby wagged his tail. This was great fun! Mrs Collins talked to the judge. He didn't look very happy. Mrs Collins kept talking to him. After a minute he nodded and gave her a small silver cup and a plastic bag. Mrs Collins walked over to Harriet and gave her the silver cup and the plastic bag. Harriet looked inside the bag and saw lots of sausages. Mrs Collins explained that the cup and the sausages were a special prize. Toby wasn't the best-trained dog, but he was certainly the cleverest!

The dog is snarling.

The dog is barking.

The dog is wagging its tail.

1. Look in the text and find the English names for the things in the photos.

1. 

....

2. 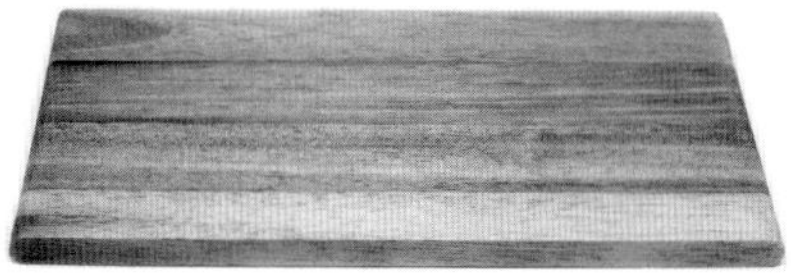

....

3. 

....

4. 

....

5. 

....

6. 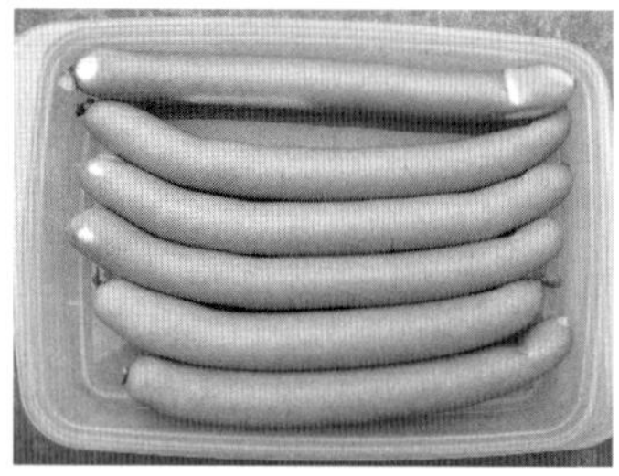

....

7. 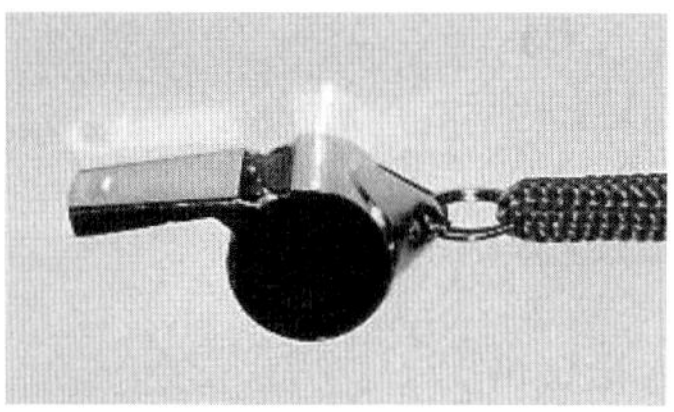

....

8. 

....

9. 

....

2. Fill in the missing prepositions.

1. I often walk .... school.
2. Dogs aren't allowed .... the shop.
3. I met my aunt and uncle .... the airport.
4. Harry invited me .... his birthday party.
5. We walked around .... circles.
6. The cat ran .... the road.
7. The horse jumped .... a fence.
8. We had .... wait over an hour for a bus home.

3. Answer the following questions about the text. Use the simple past.

1. Why didn't Toby go into the school with Harriet?

2. Who was Mrs Collins?

3. Why do you think Mrs Collins invited Harriet and Toby to the dog training club?

4. What activities at the dog training club didn't interest Toby?

5. What did interest Toby?

6. What did Harriet explain to Toby?

7. Why was Mrs Collins sceptical?

8. How did the judge start the last event?

9. What made the other dogs and their owners angry?

4. Write in the missing words from the box below.

across	at	in	into	outside	over	to	to	to	up	with

1. Today was warm and sunny, so I walked .... school.
2. I met my friend Alan .... the school gates.
3. Alan had his dog, Toby, ... him.
4. But dogs aren't allowed .... our school.
5. We went through the gates, but Toby had .... stay outside.
6. But Toby didn't stay outside. He jumped .... the wall.
7. Then he ran .... the playground.
8. He followed Alan and went .... his classroom.
9. Alan's teacher was at her desk. When she saw the dog, she stood ....
10. Alan took Toby .... and told him .... go home.

5. Find the irregular simple past forms of these verbs in the text (lines 9–30).

1. come ....
2. stand ....
3. can ....
4. see ....
5. tell ....
6. will ....
7. blow ....
8. have to *(müssen)* ....
9. run ....
10. sit ....
11. eat ....
12. give ....

Rough justice

My name is Alicia Price and I live with my Mum Roseanne on a trailer park just outside the little town of Evanston in Kentucky. I don't usually enjoy the long summer vacation because it's boring. All my school friends are away on vacation or at summer camps. My mum works in a local factory, so I'm by myself every day. This vacation is different because I have a job as a waitress in the Blue Parrot, a hamburger restaurant in Evanston. It's the only restaurant in Evanston! It gives me something to do and I can earn some money. I work from 10 a.m. to 2 p.m. and I drive there on my moped. The work isn't hard and the customers are friendly. Well, most of them – yesterday I met a customer who wasn't so nice!

I put my moped in the yard *(Hof)* behind the restaurant kitchen. I walked into the restaurant and took off my helmet and leather jacket. I walked behind the long counter *(Theke)* and hung them up in a cupboard. Michelle, the other waitress, already had her coat on. She didn't look happy. "Be careful, Alicia. The man at table 6 looks like trouble." I looked at him. He wore jeans, cowboy boots and a dirty white T-shirt and he had very short brown hair. He didn't look friendly, but there were five big men with cups of coffee at the long counter and I knew them all, so I wasn't frightened *(ich hatte keine Angst)*. Not at first, but by 10:30 a.m. I was alone behind the counter and the man at table 6 was still there.

"Hey, biker girl!" he shouted. "How about some coffee over here?" I walked over with the coffee pot and filled his cup. He lit a cigarette. I pointed to the no-smoking sign on the wall next to his table and asked him to put the cigarette out. He just laughed. Then he put his hand on the back of my knee. "Look," I told him. "I don't want any trouble. Just put out the cigarette and take your hand off my leg!" He laughed and moved his hand higher up my leg. "Now that isn't very friendly, Miss. A pretty little girl like you should be really friendly to your customers." I poured hot coffee over his hand and over the cigarette in his mouth. "I'm not a little girl and you're right – I'm not friendly!" He jumped up and now he was really, really angry. "You got a problem there, Alicia, dear?" It was Big Betty, the cook, and she was holding a big soup ladle. "You want me to come over?" The man held his hand and walked to the door. "It's OK," I told Betty. "He's leaving."

He walked outside and stopped in front of a big Harley-Davidson motorbike in front of the restaurant. He saw me watching him from the window and gave me the finger. Then he kicked the motorbike over. A very big man in a leather jacket came out of the men's restroom. His jacket had "Harley-Davidson Club" on the back. He put on his motorbike helmet and walked out of the restaurant. We heard loud shouts from outside. Betty came over to the window. "I'll call the sheriff," she said. "Tell him to be quick," I told her. "That biker is very angry!"

1. What are the English names for the things in the pictures?

1. 

2. 

3. 

4. 

5. 

6. 

7. 

8. 

9. 

10. 

11. 

12. 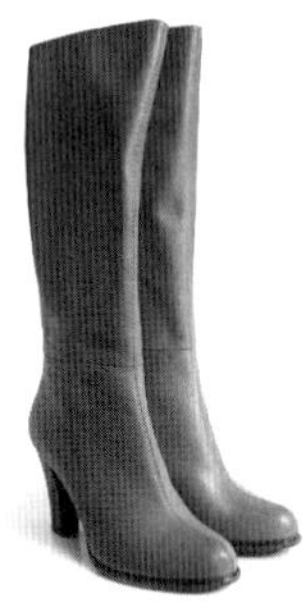

13. 

14. 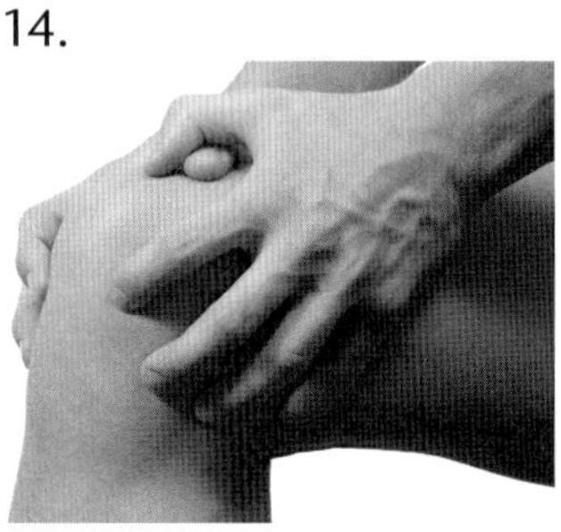

15. 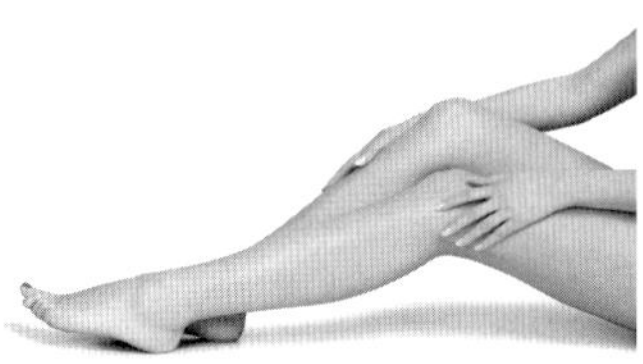

16. 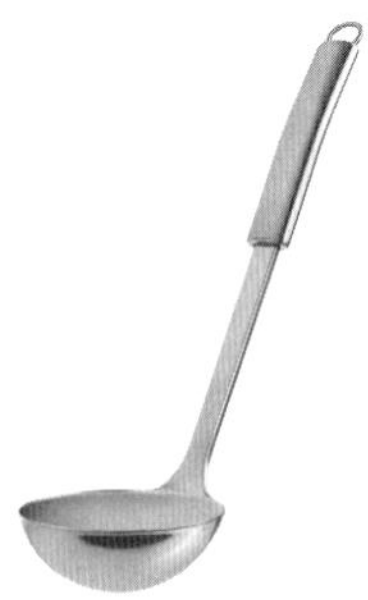

2. Explain why the man in the cowboy boots and the white T-shirt kicked over the motorbike when he left the restaurant. The words and phrases in the box below can help you.

saw / didn't see	rude / unfriendly	loud / unpleasant	argument	angry

3. Answer these questions about the text.

1. What did Michelle, the other waitress, warn Alicia about?

2. When did Alicia become frightened?

3. What did Alicia do to the man with the cigarette?

4. Who is "Big Betty" and how did she help Alicia?

5. Why did Big Betty call the sheriff?

4. Find information in the text that supports the following two statements.

1. Alicia and her mother don't have much money.

2. Evanston is a very small town.

5. Sometimes American English and British English use different names for the same things. Look up the American words in a dictionary and find the British words.

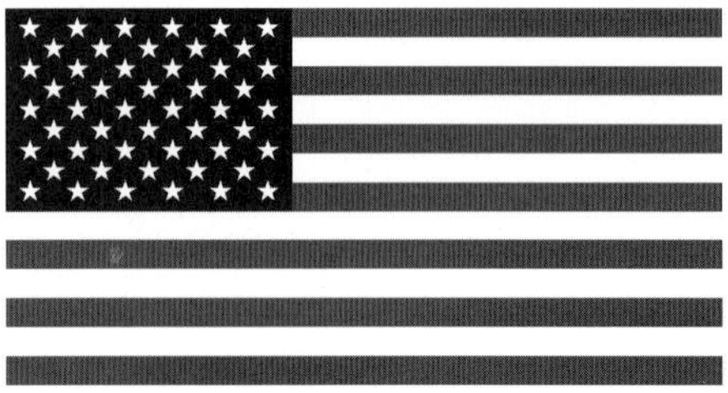

1. trailer ....
2. trailer park ....
3. vacation ....
4. restroom ....

6. Complete the sentences with the simple past forms of the verbs in brackets. All the simple past forms are in the text.

1. Yesterday Alicia .... an unpleasant customer. *(kennenlernen)*
2. The man at table 6 .... friendly. *(nicht sein)*
3. He .... like trouble! *(aussehen)*
4. He .... for some coffee. *(rufen/schreien)*
5. He .... a cigarette in the no-smoking area of the restaurant. *(anzünden)*
6. He .... his hand on Alicia's leg. *(legen)*
7. Alicia .... hot coffee over him. *(giessen, schütten)*
8. The man .... *(aufspringen)*

A smelly thug, part 1

Detective Constable Jane Hewitt looked at the old lady in the hospital bed. She looked terrible. A woman had found her lying in the street. Somebody had attacked her. A nurse was checking her pulse. "You can talk to Mrs Donelly now," she told Jane. "But only for a few minutes. She needs losts of rest *(Ruhe)*." Jane sat down and introduced herself *(stellte sich vor)*. She asked Mrs Donelly to tell her what had happened. It was a familiar story. Mrs Donelly had been to a bank in the city centre for some money. She had 500 pounds in her handbag and was on her way home. Then a young man grabbed her handbag. When she wouldn't let go of her handbag, the man had punched her in the face and when she was on the ground, he kicked *(trat)* her. Jane felt very sorry for Mrs Donelly. She was 78 and she reminded her of her own grandmother. Things like this shouldn't happen to old people. Jane was very angry, too. She really wanted to find the thug who had done this. There had been six similar attacks in the last three weeks. The attacker had chosen old people and he had attacked them from behind in places where there had been no other people and no surveillance cameras. None of the old people had been able to describe him. Jane asked Mrs Donelly if she could describe her attacker. She didn't expect *(erwartete)* to learn anything, but Mrs Donelly surprised her. "Well, I can't describe his face because I'm blind." Jane hadn't known that. "But I can tell you other things about him. He was about 25 years old, about five feet four inches tall and thin. He had just eaten a cheese and onion sandwich – I could smell it. And then he had drunk a strawberry milk shake." Jane thanked Mrs Donelly. Outside the hospital room she called her boss and told him what Mrs Donelly had said.

1. Words in context: Find the following words in the text. Read the whole sentence and then guess what the word means in German. Don't use a dictionary. Then check your answers with your classmates. Only use the dictionary if nobody knows what a word means.

1.	nurse (noun)	(line 3)	....
2.	familiar (adjective)	(line 6)	....
3.	grab (verb)	(line 8)	....
4.	punch (verb)	(line 9)	....
5.	thug (noun)	(line 12)	....
6.	similar (adjective)	(line 13)	....
7.	surveillance camera (noun)	(line 15)	....
8.	none (pronoun)	(line 15)	....
9.	onion (noun)	(line 20)	....
10.	strawberry (noun)	(line 20)	....

2. Look in the text and find the past perfect forms of the following verbs.

1. find ....
2. attack ....
3. tell ....
4. sit ....
5. ask ....
6. happen ....
7. be ....
8. punch ....
9. feel ....
10. do ....
11. choose ....
12. know ....
13. eat ....
14. drink ....

3. Write down the information that Mrs Donelly gave Jane about her attacker. Use the Internet or a dictionary and convert *(wandle um)* the British measurements *(Maße)* of height (feet and inches) into centimetres.

Mrs Donelly's attacker:

gender: male

age:

height in inches (1 foot = 12 inches):

height in centimetres:

weight:

Other information:

4. Answer these questions about the text.

1. Why did the man attack Mrs Donelly?

2. What had her attacker done?

3. Why is the policewoman so angry?

4. How did Mrs Donelly surprise the policewoman?

5. Imagine you are a police officer. How would you use Mrs Donelly's information to find her attacker?

A smelly thug, part 2

D. C. Jane Hewitt met her boss, Detective Sergeant Preston at the crime scene *(Tatort)* in the city centre. They walked from there to Mrs Donelly's bank. She had collected 500 pounds at 3:52 p.m. the day before. There was a sandwich shop with a big window right across the street. They walked inside and D. S. Preston looked at the sandwiches behind the counter.

"Two cheese and onion sandwiches, please. Do you do milk shakes?"

"Yes," the assistant said. "What would you like: vanilla, chocolate or strawberry?"

"What do you fancy, Jane?"

"I'll have a cup of tea, please, Sarge."

"Right, me too. Two teas, please, Miss." He showed the girl his police badge *(Polizeimarke)*.

"Were you here yesterday afternoon between three o'clock and four o'clock?"

"Yes, I was. How can I help you?"

"Can you remember a young man who bought a cheese and onion sandwich and a strawberry milkshake?"

"No, but I can look at yesterday's sales." She went to the till *(Kasse)* and pressed some buttons *(Tasten)*. "Here it is. An onion sandwich with a strawberry milkshake. The time on the receipt *(Beleg)* is 3:53 p.m. Do you want a copy?"

"Yes, thanks. Well, we know that he was here. Perhaps we can find a customer who was also here yesterday at that time and remembers the man."

"Why don't you just look at the photos?" the assistant told them. She pointed to a small box on the back wall of the shop. "It takes a high definition *(hochauflösend)* photo of the shop every 20 seconds. You can use the computer in the office."

Ten minutes later Jane e-mailed a photo of the thug and a description of the crime to every police officer in the city.

Jane visited Mrs Donelly at the hospital the next morning. She gave her some flowers and told her that thanks to her description they had found the thief very quickly. An hour after her e-mail Jane had got a call from a policeman who had recognized the man in the photo and knew his name and his address. She and her boss had arrested the man at his home just half an hour later. He still had 450 pounds in his pocket and they had found Mrs Donelly's handbag under his bed.

6. Rewrite the story as a play in your exercise book. The scene cards below can help you.

Scene 1 Place: A hospital room 3 Roles: D. C. Hewitt, nurse, Mrs Donelly	**Scene 2** Place: Crime scene in city centre 2 Roles: D. C. Hewitt, D. S. Preston	**Scene 3** Place: A bank 3 Roles: D. C. Hewitt, D. S. Preston, bank manager
Scene 4 Place: A sandwich shop 3 Roles: D. C. Hewitt, D. S. Preston, assistant	**Scene 5** Place: attacker's home 3 Roles: D. C. Hewitt, D. S. Preston, attacker	**Scene 6** Place: A hospital room 2 Roles: D. C. Hewitt, Mrs Donelly

7. Complete the sentences with information from the text.

1. Jane Hewitt is a ....
2. She is visiting .... in hospital.
3. Mrs Donelly is lying in a hospital bed because ....
....
4. A nurse was ....
5. The nurse told Jane that she could only ....
6. This was because Mrs Donelly ....
7. A young man .... Mrs Donelly near the bank.
8. He .... her handbag with 500 pounds in it.
9. She ...., so he punched her in the face and kicked her.
10. Jane felt very sorry for Mrs Donelly because ....
....
11. Jane hadn't known that Mrs Donelly ....
12. Mrs Donelly told Jane that her attacker ....
....
13. When Jane and her boss went back to the crime scene, they saw ....
....
14. The assistant in the sandwich shop gave the detectives a ....
15. .... at 3:53 p.m. the day before.
16. The assistant told the detectives about the .... and the detectives soon found a .... of Mrs Donelly's attacker.

Two car hijacks, case #1

You won't see many convertibles *(Cabrios)* in Miami for two very good reasons. Firstly, it's simply too hot – driver and passengers would be suffering from sunstroke after only half an hour or so. Secondly, it's too easy to steal and that can be very dangerous if you are sitting in the car at the time! European tourists who ignore *(nicht beachten)* this can end up either in a hospital or in the morgue.

So when Juan Hernandez and his friend Carlos Guzman saw this beautiful Maserati® stop at a traffic light in front of the bar where they were drinking, they thought Christmas had arrived early. They walked over to the car and opened the doors. They were even polite about it. Perhaps they had read the leaflet from the Miami Tourist Board about being nice to tourists. Carlos took the key from the ignition and stepped back so that the driver could get out of the car, which he did very quickly when he saw the very big revolver in the belt of Carlos's jeans. Juan held the door open for the woman passenger, bowed *(verbeugte sich)* politely and said "Gracias, Senora." They closed the car doors, Carlos put the key back into the ignition *(Zündung)* and started the engine.

The traffic light turned green, but when Carlos stepped on the accelerator pedal, nothing happened. The Maserati® didn't have an automatic transmission like American cars. It had a European stick shift *(Gangschaltung)* and neither Carlos nor Juan had ever used one before. They were still arguing about how it worked when the police arrived.

> When a thief steals an empty car, that is **theft**. If there is somebody in the car when a thief steals it (a driver or a passenger), that is a **hijack**, which is a more serious *(schwereres)* crime.

1. Which words from the text are these definitions describing?

1. A person who is travelling in a vehicle *(Fahrzeug)*, but isn't driving it.

   ....

2. This is an illness with fever and headaches which people get if they have stayed out too long in the hot sun, especially if they haven't worn a hat.

   ....

3. This is a special room or a building for the bodies of people who die in hospital or in an accident.

   ....

2. Complete these sentences with words from the text.

1. Miami has got a very .... climate.
2. .... aren't popular cars in Miami.
3. Miami can be a dangerous place for .... who don't take care.
4. The Miami Tourist Board prints a .... which asks people in Miami to be friendly to tourists.
5. The text is about a car ....
6. The hijackers in the text were friendly and they even behaved ....
7. Most American cars have an automatic ....
8. Many Americans have never used a .... shift.

3. Find the words in the text which have the same meanings as the following German words. Don't use a German-English dictionary.
Afterwards check your answers with your classmates.

1. Gründe .... (line ....)
2. Broschüre .... (line ....)
3. stehlen .... (line ....)
4. Verkehrsampel .... (line ....)
5. Weihnachten .... (line ....)
6. höflich .... (line ....)
7. Schlüssel .... (line ....)
8. Automatikschaltung .... (line ....)
9. Gürtel .... (line ....)
10. Motor .... (line ....)
11. Gaspedal .... (line ....)

Two car hijacks, case #2

Boston businessman Edward Candy left the restaurant at 10:40 p.m. and got into his new metallic silver Mercedes for the short drive home. At 10:55 p.m. his mobile phone signalled that he had received a text message. Mr Candy pulled his car to the curb and stopped so that he could read his text message. Then a man knocked *(klopfte)* on his side window and said something that Mr Candy didn't hear properly. Without thinking, he lowered the window – and saw a big handgun pointed at him. The man told him to unlock the doors and not to do anything stupid. Then he opened the door and got into the front passenger seat. Another man got into the rear seat *(Rücksitz)*. The man in the front told Mr Candy to drive. This was the start of a two-hour nightmare for Mr Candy.

The man in the back wanted to drive to a quiet side street where they could shoot Mr Candy, but the other man said that he felt tired and didn't feel like driving and it was good to have a driver – at least for a while. They discussed where they wanted to go and decided to drive to New York. The man in the back said he was hungry and they should get something to eat first. They decided to get hamburgers and milkshakes at a drive-in restaurant and told Mr Candy to drive to Fordham Road. When they came to the drive-in window, the man in front held his gun behind Mr Candy's back and told him what to order. Mr Candy paid for the food and they drove on. While they ate, the men looked through Mr Candy's wallet. They were both very angry that there was now only about 12 dollars in cash and the man in front pressed his gun to Mr Candy's head. Mr Candy told them that he had two bank cards and could collect 500 dollars in cash with each one. The man in the back said that there was a drive-through bank on Commonwealth Avenue and he told Mr Candy how to get there.

They collected the money and that made both men much happier. They told Mr Candy to drive them to New York. He warned them that the tank was nearly empty and they would need to buy diesel before the long drive to New York. The man in the back checked the fuel gauge *(Tankanzeige)* on the dashboard. "OK. Turn right here into Memorial Drive, there's a gas station on the right." Then he turned to the man in the front and whispered, "And I'll drive on from there." Mr Candy knew that they would kill him there. "I don't want to die," he thought. "Not like this!" He decided that he would do something, even if it was very dangerous. When they stopped in front of the diesel pump *(Zapfsäule)*, they saw a big sign:

CASH ONLY AFTER MIDNIGHT – AND IN ADVANCE!

The man in the back shouted, "Shit!" The two men argued about who should get out and pay. "I've got the gun!" the man in the front said and won the argument. The man in the back swore again, but he got out and walked over to the Food Mart to pay. The man in the front told Mr Candy to switch on the satnav *(Navi)* and enter an address in New York. Mr Candy thought that this could be his chance to escape *(fliehen)*. He told the man that the car was new and he didn't know how to use the satnav. The man put his gun in the door pocket and began to enter an address in New York. Very quickly Mr Candy opened his seat belt *(Sicherheitsgurt)* and his door and jumped out of the car. He ran away from the car and behind the petrol pumps so that the man in the car couldn't shoot him so easily. He ran across a road to another gas station and ran to the cash desk and shouted to the assistant to lock the doors and call 911.

The police arrived eight minutes later in three cars and Mr Candy's nightmare ended. Both hijackers were gone, but his Mercedes was still there and his wallet was on the passenger seat. The police took the details and told Mr Candy that he was a very lucky man – the hijack had only cost him a 1,000 dollars and not his life. Mr Candy agreed.

4. Fill in the crossword puzzle with the English translations.
Note: If the English word consists of two words, there is no space between words in the crossword.

Across
4. Essen
6. Bargeld
8. Kopf
9. Treibstoff
10. Hinweistafel
11. müde
13. Streit
14. Geschäftsmann
16. entriegeln/aufschließen
17. leer
18. Fahrt
19. Bordsteinkante

Down
1. im Voraus
2. Brieftasche
3. Mitternacht
5. gefährlich
7. Armaturenbrett
8. Handfeuerwaffe
12. Albtraum
15. Silber

5. Fill in the missing prepositions.

1. Something is knocking .... the side of the car.
2. I don't have a satnav, so I asked my friend .... read the map.
3. I don't like it when strangers point guns .... me!
4. We drove .... a quiet restaurant.
5. On a long journey it's good .... have a passenger.

6. Answer these questions about the text. Use full sentences.

1. Where does the story take place? ....

2. Where had Mr Candy just been? ....

3. Why did Mr Candy pull his car to the curb and stop? ....

....

4. What did Mr Candy do when someone knocked on the side window of his car?

....

....

5. Why was this the wrong thing to do? ....

....

6. What did the hijackers first want to do? ....

....

7. Why did they change their minds *(ihre Meinung ändern)*? ....

....

8. Why did the two hijackers get angry with Mr Candy? ....

....

9. Why did the hijackers tell Mr Candy to stop at the gas station? ....

....

10. Why did one of the hijackers leave the car? ....

....

11. Where did Mr Candy run to when he escaped from the car? ....

....

12. How long had Mr Candy's nightmare lasted? ....

....

Heartless crimes, part 1: A burglary

Last Thursday two burglars broke into Mr Albert Culper's home in Eston while he was at his wife's funeral. His dead wife's jewellery, a fur coat, a laptop computer, a television set and a video recorder were among the things stolen. But the thieves also ransacked *(durchwühlen)* Mr Culper's home. When he and his daughter returned home from the funeral, they found that their home had been destroyed. Their furniture had been smashed *(zertrümmert)*, books had been ripped apart *(auseinandergerissen)*, the contents *(Inhalt)* of drawers and cupboards had been thrown onto the floor and carpets, walls and windows had been smeared with paint. When he saw the damage, Mr Culper, 67, collapsed and was rushed to hospital. A hospital spokeswoman later described his condition *(Zustand)* as "serious *(ernst)*, but not critical".

Mr Culper's daughter Tracey, 28, described the burglars as "heartless animals". Yesterday Detective Sergeant Kevin Oakham described the crime scene in Teesside Crown Court. "I was shocked. It was really vicious. The house looked as if it had been hit by a bomb. The thieves had kicked in a door. They had smashed every piece of furniture in every room, upstairs and downstairs. The floors were covered in broken glass, cups, plates and food from the cupboards and the fridge. The burglars weren't in a hurry and they didn't try to be quiet. They must have known that everyone in the street would be at Mrs Culper's funeral." Detective Sergeant Oakham told the judge how he had caught one of the burglars. "Tracey, Mr Culper's daughter, gave me a list of everyone who had been invited to the funeral. There was only one person on the list who hadn't been at the funeral. Her name was Claire Boswell, a neighbour who lived in the same street. When I learned that Mrs Boswell was a drug addict *(Drogenabhängiger)*, I and four police officers searched her house. We found gloves, an anorak and a pair of jeans with traces *(Spuren)* of the same paint that had been used in Mr Culper's house. Boswell admitted that she had been one of the burglars, but she wouldn't give us the name of her accomplice."

Tracey Culper said, "I'm disgusted at what she has done. My mother and our other neighbours were good to her. We all felt sorry for her and we tried to help her get off the drugs. We looked after her when she was ill, took her to the hospital for therapy, bought food for her and cooked meals for her. We all tried to help her and this is what she does to us!"

Claire Boswell, 24, was found guilty *(schuldig)* of burglary and vandalism and was sent to prison for ten months. Tracey Culper thought that the prison sentence *(Haftstrafe)* was much too lenient. "It's laughable! She'll be free in six or seven months. This was a really despicable crime. I think the judge must live on a different planet than the rest of us."

1. Label the things in the photos with words from the text.

1. 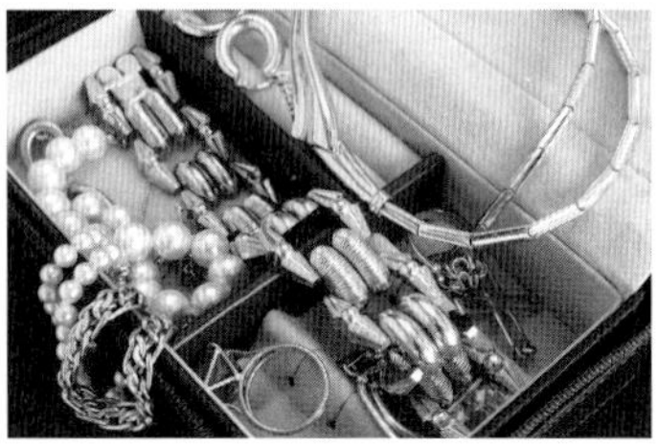

....

2. 

....

3. 

....

4. 

....

5. 

....

6. 

....

7. 

....

8. 

....

9. 

....

2. Words in context: Find these words in the text. Underline or highlight what you think is the best translation. Check your results in an English-German dictionary.

1. heartless (kopflos • herzlos • wild)
2. vicious (boshaft • unbarmherzig • komisch)
3. disgusted (erstaunt • angewidert • genervt)
4. lenient (bequem • leicht • milde)
5. laughable (humorvoll • lächerlich • albern)
6. despicable (verachtenswert • gemein • sauer)

3. Answer these questions about the text. Keep your answers as short as possible.

1. Who was burgled?

2. When did the burglary happen?

3. What was stolen?

4. What other things did the burglars do?

5. How was one of the burglars caught?

6. Why was Tracey Culper so disgusted with Claire Boswell?

7. Why was Tracey Culper angry with the judge?

8. Do you agree or disagree with Tracey? Why?

4. Change the active simple past sentences below into passive sentences. The examples in the box can help you. All the verbs are used in the text.

infinitive verb form	**passive form of the simple past**
know	was/were known
sell	was/were sold
build	was/were built

1. A thief broke into the supermarket.

2. Vandals ransacked *(plünderten)* the building.

3. The police found some spray cans.

4. The fire destroyed everything in the shop.

5. Somebody smashed a window.

6. Somebody kicked in the door.

7. The paramedics *(Sanitäter)* rushed the man to hospital.

8. A neighbour gave the police the number of the van.

9. The burglar used a hammer.

5. The suffix -less can be used with many words. Guess the meaning of these words.

1. jobless ....
2. thoughtless ....
3. endless ....
4. timeless ....
5. priceless ....
6. homeless ....
7. lifeless ....
8. helpless ....
9. hopeless ....

6. Read the text again and then complete the sentences with suitable words.

While Mr Culper, his .... (1) Tracey and his neighbours attended his wife's .... (2), his home was burgled. Claire Boswell, 24, was .... (3) of the thieves. The young woman was a drug .... (4) who lived in the same street. The police suspected *(verdächtigte)* her because she hadn't been at the funeral although she had been .... (5). She and an .... (6) had ransacked Mr Culper's house. They destroyed furniture and books, ... (7) cups and plates, threw food on the floor and sprayed .... (8) over everything. The house looked as though a .... (9) had hit it. Mr Culper had to be taken to .... (10) and even the police were shocked. The police searched Claire Boswell's house and found the .... (11) she had worn during the burglary. She wouldn't tell the police the .... (12) of the other burglar. The judge sent her to .... (13) for ten months.

Heartless crimes, part 2: A hit-and-run

The Mitchells were a farming family. Mr Albert Mitchell, his wife Gloria and his sons Alan and Ralph lived together with Mr Mitchell's brother, Ted, his wife Edith and daughter Rosemary in a big old farmhouse near the village of Normanby in Cleveland. Twice a week, on Tuesday and Friday afternoons the women of the family took the landrover and drove to Scarborough about 50 miles away on the coast. Gloria Mitchell visited her mother, who lived there. Edith and Rosemary went shopping. At seven o'clock on these evenings Albert, Alan, Ralph and Ted walked the half a mile from their farm to The Black Bull, the village pub. They were popular there. They were all tall, strong men, but very friendly. They drank two or three beers, played darts and chatted with their friends and around ten o'clock they walked home.

At 10:30 p.m. on Wednesday, May 10, 1965, a motorist dialled 999 from a telephone box and reported a serious accident with some people injured *(verletzt)*. The emergency call was passed to the police station in Normanby and Police Constable Gregory Merton drove to the scene of the accident on his motorbike. He found the motorist who had made the call on his knees in front of a man lying by the side of the road. The motorist had covered the man with a blanket and was holding his hand and talking to him. P. C. Merton saw three more men lying at the side of the road. He recognized three of the Mitchells – Albert, Ralph and Ted. They weren't breathing and he couldn't find a pulse. Alan was still alive, but he was very badly injured. Then the ambulance arrived.

From paint flakes *(Splitter)* at the scene, the police knew that the colour of the hit-and-run car was green. They interviewed everyone in the area who had a green car, but the hit-and-run driver was never found. Alan Mitchell left the hospital six months later in a wheelchair. He would never walk again. Gregory Merton never forgot that scene of horror. In his long career as a policeman it remained the worst hit-and-run crime that he had ever seen. He married a local girl and they remained in Normanby after his retirement. One of Gregory's hobbies was local history and he had a website about local history. When Alan Mitchell died in 2011, Gregory wrote about the unsolved *(ungelöst)* hit-and-run crime. Six months later he got an e-mail from a woman in New Zealand. In 1965 she had been twelve years old and had lived with her parents in Durham, a town about 30 miles from Normanby. She remembered her father talking about his cousin in Normanby. His cousin had asked him for help. If the police asked, he wanted her father to tell them that he had been at his birthday party and hadn't left until after 11 p.m. She remembered that her mother had told her father not to do it. Her father's birthday was May 10 and the cousin's name was Terry Brewster. Gregory Merton looked through the old case file *(Fallakte)*. A Mr Terence Brewster had been interviewed by one of his police colleagues. Mr Brewster had owned a green van. This had been examined and no damage had been found. On the evening of May 10 Mr Brewster had told the police that he had been helping his brother-in-law, Bill Summers, on his farm in Stokesly, ten miles away and that he had stayed overnight. The police had checked this with Mr Summers and he had confirmed *(bestätigt)* it. Gregory Merton drove to the Summer's small farm in Stokesly. Bill Summers had been dead for five years, but his widow *(Witwe)* remembered. Her brother had paid them 800 pounds for the alibi and he had left his old van with them. She took Gregory to an old shed behind the farmhouse and showed him an old green van. The front of the van was badly damaged. Mrs Summers told Gregory that her brother had gone to Edmonton in Canada 40 years ago and she had never heard from him since then.

When Gregory told his wife about it, she told him to leave it, he had done enough. "Who will it help? All the Mitchells are dead and if Terry Brewster is still alive, he'll be an old man."

7. Label the things in the photos with words from the text.

1. 

....

2. 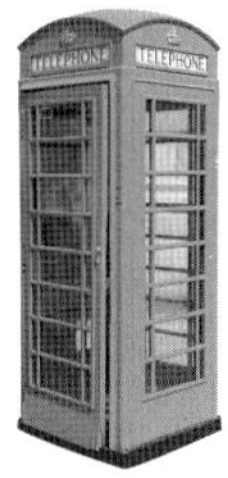

....

3. 

....

4. 

....

5. 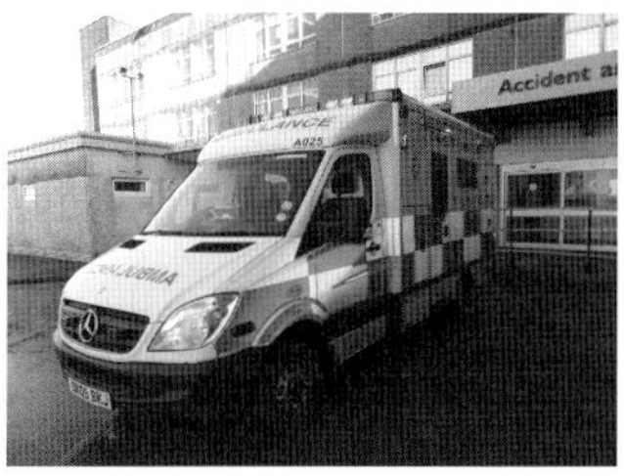

....

6. 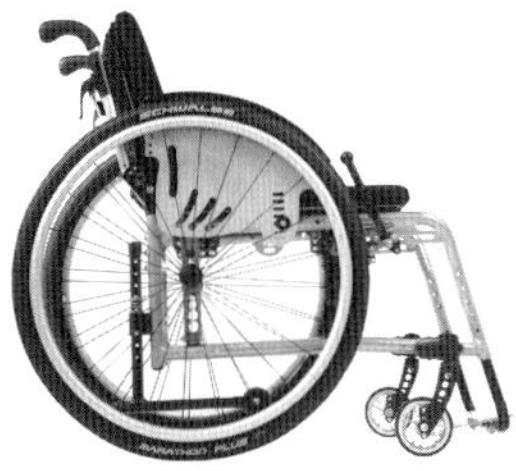

....

7. 

....

8. 

....

8. Complete the sentences with a word from the text.

1. The two Mitchell families lived .... in a big farmhouse.
2. Scarborough is a town on the ....
3. The Black Bull in Normanby was the .... pub.
4. The men of the Mitchell family walked to the pub .... a week.
5. If someone doesn't have a ...., they are probably dead.
6. Alan Mitchell didn't die, but he was badly ....

9. Complete the following definitions with information from the text.

1. ………………………… is a popular pub game in many countries.
2. The ………………………… telephone number in the United Kingdom is 999.
3. A ………………………… is when a driver doesn't stop after an accident.
4. A ………………………… comes at the end of a person's career when they stop working and live on a pension.
5. A ………………………… is the son or the daughter of an aunt or an uncle.
6. A ………………………… is somebody who works with you.

10. Are these statements about the text true (T) or false (F)? Correct the false sentences.

1. The Mitchells worked for a farmer in Normanby. ……………
2. Gloria, Edith and Rosemary Mitchell drove to Scarborough twice a week. ……………
3. Ralph Mitchel was a small, unfriendly man. ……………
4. A motorist was the first person at the crime scene. ……………
5. The paramedics with the ambulance were the next people at the scene. ……………
6. Gregory Merton got a letter from a woman in New Zealand. ……………
7. The woman from New Zealand had once lived in Normanby. ……………
8. Mrs Summers was Terry Brewster's sister. ……………
9. Mrs Merton wanted her husband to find Terry Brewster in Canada. ……………

Corrections:

…………………………………………………………………………………………

…………………………………………………………………………………………

…………………………………………………………………………………………

…………………………………………………………………………………………

…………………………………………………………………………………………

…………………………………………………………………………………………

Lösungen

An expensive trap (page 5–6)

1. 1. Erde/Boden 2. bis 3. (zer)brechen 4. Stück(chen)
5. Verdammt!/Verflucht! 6. fluchen 7. bezahlt 8. Radarwarnanlage
9. funktionieren 10. Reifen

2. 1. plastic box 2. suitcase 3. roof rack 4. window
5. brake light 6. bumper 7. tyre 8. hubcap
9. bag

Three liars: A sketch (page 7–10)

1. 1. has got 2. is, isn't 3. thinks 4. doesn't want
5. shows 6. tests, asks 7. lies, buzzes

2. 1. T 2. N 3. F 4. T 5. N 6. T 7. F 8. N

3. Individual solution

4a) 1. Hauskatze 2. Hausmann 3. Hausfrau 4. Haushalt
5. Hausarbeit 6. Haushälter 7. Hausbesitzer 8. Einbrecher

4b) 1. Hausaufgabe(n) 2. obdachlos 3. selbst gemacht 4. Eigenheimbesitzer
5. krank vor Heimweh 6. Heimatstadt 7. Heimarbeiter 8. Heimat(land)

5. 1. Meine Mutter arbeitet zu Hause. Sie ist Heimarbeiterin.
2. Mein Computer funktioniert/geht nicht. Ich glaube, er ist kaputt.

A serial killer (page 11–13)

1. 1. around 2. to 3. at 4. up 5. got

2. 1. serial 2. murders 3. addresses 4. morning 5. cereal(s)
6. muesli 7. pallet 8. bath 9. milk 10. cereal

3. People with dogs must have a dog licence from the town hall. The police can ask the town hall for a list of people with brown dogs. The killer sends letters by post, so the killer must send the letter to the police by 4:15 p.m. on the day before a new murder. The police can watch the people with brown dogs and wait for one of them to post a letter in a letter box.

4. 1E 2D 3B 4C 5A

5. Individual solution

6. Individual solution

Two swinders (page 14–15)

1. 1. playground 2. lend 3. pocket money 4. mobile phone
5. offer 6. think 7. swindler 8. favourite subject
9. lose 10. agree

2. 1. Ich weiß es auch nicht. 2. Das geschieht dir recht.

3. 1. She wants to buy a mobile phone card.
2. She needs five pounds.
3. They agree to have a quiz about animals for money.
4. Tony thinks he can't lose because he knows a lot about animals (It's his favourite subject).
5. She describes an animal, but there is no animal like this.

4. Individual solution

Case 273 (page 16–19)

1. 1. door 2. key 3. window 4. breathing mask
5. plate 6. tin 7. bottle 8. (Gorgonzola) cheese

2. Across
5. bottles [Flaschen]
7. police station [Polizeiwache]
9. window [Fenster]
11. neighbour [Nachbarin]
15. wounds [Wunden]
17. key service [Schluesseldienst]
18. beans [Bohnen]
19. midnight [Mitternacht]
20. file [Akte]

Down
1. key [Schluessel]
2. body [Leiche]
3. plate [Teller]
4. breathing mask [Atemschutzmaske]
6. slices [Scheiben]
8. crime scene [Tatort]
10. bedroom [Schlafzimmer]
12. meal [Mahlzeit]
13. tins [Dosen]
14. bad smell [Gestank]
15. flat [Wohnung]
16. death [Tod]

3. 176.9

4. The flat was locked. All the windows were closed and locked. There were no wounds on the body.

5. Individual solution; bad smell, enormous meal of beans, Gorgonzola cheese and beer

6. 1. Obduktion/Autopsie 2. Ergebnisse/Befund 3. raten/erraten 4. Herzanfall/Herzinfarkt
5. Methangas 6. Kohlendioxid 7. tödlich 8. Giftgas
9. erzeugen/produzieren 10. verdauen

Multitasking (page 20–22)

1. 1. river 2. police officer 3. driving licence 4. bottle
5. bridge 6. crowd

2. Individual solution

3. 1. from 2. with 3. across 4. over
5. in 6. at 7. into 8. for

4. 1. in front of – behind, hinter 2. strong – weak, schwach 3. empty – full, voll
4. back seat – front seat, Vordersitz 5. important – unimportant, unwichtig
6. mad – sane, zurechnungsfähig/bei gesundem Verstand 7. difficult – easy, einfach/leicht
8. take off (clothes) – put on (clothes), (Kleidung) anziehen

5. 1. injured 2. driver, didn't have 3. wife of a government minister
4. mad killer 5. having a baby, for help 6. driver of the bus

The cheeky shoplifter (page 23–27)

1. 1. lipstick 2. sweater 3. coat 4. nail varnish
5. blouse 6. skirt 7. jacket 8. mascara
9. watch 10. shopping bag

2. 1. expensive 2. cosmetics 3. ladies' toilet 4. cash desk
5. cheap 6. receipts 7. steal 8. stolen
9. fat 10. leather

3. 1. around 2. at 3. to 4. in/into
5. on 6. back 7. for

4. 1. Store detectives must wait until a customer leaves the shop without paying for something before they can stop him or her and call the police.
2. A store detective can stop a customer and ask to look in his or her bag, but only a police officer can search somebody and arrest him or her.
3. The policewoman had to let the girl go because she was only twelve and she had receipts for the things in her shopping bag.
4. The girl had given the stolen clothes and cosmetics to another person when she was in the ladies' toilet.
5. Another person bought the T-shirts and gave them and the receipts to the girl in the ladies' toilet.
6. She asked another store detective to help her. She followed the girl and the other store detective waited outside the ladies' toilet and checked the women who came out.

5. 1. was/were 2. saw 3. put 4. went
5. waited 6. came 7. watched 8. ran
9. stopped 10. took 11. called 12. arrived

6. 1. C+D 2. E 3. A+C 4. A 5. B
6. Sie sollen nur die Sachen stehlen, die der Laden nicht verkaufen kann.
7. Sie drohen, Ladendiebe zu ‚beenden'.
8. Es ist (hoffentlich) nicht ernst gemeint.

<u>Two smugglers (page 28–32)</u>

1. 1. harbour 2. passport 3. ferry 4. unpack
5. blouse 6. leather 7. drugs 8. colleagues
9. smuggler 10. market

2. 1. H 2. E 3. G 4. C 5. I 6. A 7. D 8. J 9. B 10. F

3. 1. Haben Sie etwas zu verzollen? 2. Bitte packen Sie Ihre Rücksäcke aus.

4. They were smuggling backpacks.

5. Possible solution:
1. They travelled on the ferry from Algeciras in Spain to Tangier in Morocco in the morning and they returned on the ferry from Tangier to Algeciras in the evening.
2. It's unusual to make the long round trip on the same day.
3. They found old/used clothes.

6. shake – shook, have – had, be – was/were, leave – left, make – made, tell – told, think – thought, can't – couldn't, find – found, go – went, see – saw

7. 4. find – found 5. let – let 6. make – made 7. tell – told
8. leave – left 9. think – thought 10. go – went 11. see – saw

8. 1. were checked 2. were asked 3. were noted 4. were searched
5. was found 6. was solved 7. were seen

9. Individual solution

The clever sausage thief (page 33–36)

1. 1. gate 2. plank 3. wall 4. fence
5. basket 6. sausages 7. whistle 8. cup
9. plastic bag

2. 1. to 2. in 3. at 4. to
5. in 6. across 7. over 8. to

3. 1. Toby didn't go past the school gates because animals weren't allowed in the school.
2. Mrs Collins was Harriet's English teacher.
3. Mrs Collins also had a dog and she thought it would interest Harriet and Toby.
4. Toby wasn't interested in walking around in circles, running over planks, jumping over walls and fences.
5. The contest (where the dogs had to wait for their owners to tell them to eat their sausages) interested Toby.
6. Harriet explained the rules of the contest to Toby.
7. Mrs Collins didn't think that dogs really understood what their owners said.
8. The judge blew his whistle and started the event.
9. Toby ran down the line of dogs and ate their sausages.

4. 1. to 2. at 3. with 4. in
5. to 6. over 7. across 8. into
9. up 10. outside, to

5. 1. came 2. stood 3. could 4. saw
5. told 6. would 7. blew 8. had to
9. ran 10. sat 11. ate 12. gave

Rough justice (page 37–40)

1. 1. trailer (BE: caravan) 2. factory 3. waitress 4. money
5. moped 6. customer 7. motorbike 8. (motorbike) helmet
9. (motorbike) jacket 10. cupboard 11. coat 12. boots
13. sign 14. knee 15. leg 16. (soup) ladle

2. Possible solution: When the man in the cowboy boots and the white T-shirt saw Alicia arrive in the restaurant, she was wearing a biker jacket and a motorbike helmet. He didn't see her moped. When he left the restaurant, he was angry with Alicia and he kicked over the motorbike because he thought it belonged to her.

3. 1. Michelle warned her that one of the customers looked like trouble.
2. Alicia became frightened after 10:30 a.m. because she was now alone.
3. She poured hot coffee over his hand and the cigarette in his mouth.
4. "Big Betty" was the cook and the man was frightened because she was big and she had a big ladle.
5. Big Betty called the sheriff because the Harley-Davidson biker was big and very angry with the man who had kicked over his motorbike.

4. 1. Alicia and her mother live on a trailer park (BE: caravan site). They can't afford a vacation (BE: holiday) or a summer camp for Alicia. Alicia needs money and must work for it.
2. Evanston must be a small town because it only has one restaurant.

5. 1. caravan 2. caravan site 3. holiday(s) 4. toilet(s)

6. 1. met 2. wasn't 3. looked 4. shouted
5. lit 6. put 7. poured 8. jumped up

A smelly thug (page 41–45)

1.
1. Krankenschwester
2. gewohnt/bekannt
3. packen/schnappen/ergreifen
4. mit der Faust schlagen
5. Rowdy/Schläger
6. ähnlich
7. Überwachungskamera
8. keiner/keine/keines
9. Zwiebel
10. Erdbeere

2. 1. had found 2. had attacked 3. had told 4. had sat
5. had asked 6. had happened 7. had been 8. had punched
9. had felt 10. had done 11. had chosen 12. had known
13. had eaten 14. had drunk

3. age: about 25; height: 5 feet 4 inches = 64 inches = 163 centimetres; weight: thin; other information: had just eaten a cheese and onion sandwich, had drunk a strawberry milkshake

4.
1. He knew that Mrs Donelly had money in her handbag and she was alone.
2. Her attacker had punched her in the face and then he had kicked her when she was on the ground.
3. The policewoman is angry because things like this shouldn't happen to old people. There had also been other attacks in the last 3 weeks.
4. The other old people hadn't been able to describe their attackers. Mrs Donelly is blind, but she describes her attacker exactly.

5. Go back to the crime scene. Look for places near there that sell cheese and onion sandwiches and/or strawberry milkshakes. Ask assistants for a description. Find a surveillance camera.

6. Individual solution

7.
1. detective constable/detective/police officer
2. Mrs Donelly/an old lady/an old woman
3. somebody/someone/a man had attacked her the day before
4. checking Mrs Donelly's pulse
5. stay for a few minutes/a short time
6. needed lots of rest
7. had attacked
8. had grabbed
9. wouldn't let go of the handbag
10. she was 78 and reminded her of her own grandmother (and things like that shouldn't happen to old people)
11. was blind
12. had eaten a cheese and onion sandwich and had drunk a strawberry milkshake
13. a sandwich shop with a big window across the street
14. receipt
15. Mrs Donelly's attacker/A young man had been there
16. surveillance camera, photo

Two car hijacks (page 46–50)

1. 1. passenger 2. sunstroke 3. morgue

2. 1. hot 2. Convertibles 3. tourists 4. leaflet
5. hijack 6. politely 7. transmission 8. stick

3. 1. reasons (line 1) 2. leaflet (line 9) 3. steal (line 3) 4. traffic light (line 7)
5. Christmas (line 8) 6. polite (line 9) 7. key (line 10) 8. automatic transmission (line 17)
9. belt (line 12) 10. engine (line 15) 11. accelerator pedal

4. Across

4. food (Essen)
6. cash (Bargeld)
8. head (Kopf)
9. fuel (Treibstoff)
10. sign (Hinweistafel)
11. tired (müde)
13. argument (Streit)
14. businessman (Geschäftsmann)
16. unlock (entriegeln/aufschließen)
17. empty (leer)
18. drive (Fahrt)
19. curb (Bordsteinkante)

Down

1. in advance (im Voraus)
2. wallet (Brieftasche)
3. midnight (Mitternacht)
5. dangerous (gefährlich)
7. dashboard (Armaturenbrett)
8. handgun (Handfeuerwaffe)
12. nightmare (Albtraum)
15. silver (Silber)

5. 1. on 2. to 3. at 4. to 5. to

6.
1. The story takes place in Boston, USA.
2. Mr Candy had just been to a restaurant.
3. Mr Candy stopped because his mobile had just received a text message and he wanted to read it.
4. When somebody knocked on the side window, Mr Candy lowered the window.
5. This was the wrong thing to do because the man outside was a hijacker and now he could point his gun through the open window.
6. They wanted to drive somewhere quiet and shoot Mr Candy.
7. They changed their minds because one of them said he felt tired and he didn't want to drive.
8. Both hijackers got angry with Mr Candy because he didn't have much money in his wallet.
9. The hijackers told Mr Candy to stop at the gas station because they wanted to fill the tank of the car for the long drive to New York.
10. One of the hijackers had to leave the car and go to the Food Mart and pay in cash in advance.
11. When he escaped from the car, Mr Candy ran to another gas station across the road.
12. Mr Candy's nightmare had lasted for two hours.

Heartless crimes (page 51–58)

1. 1. jewellery 2. fur coat 3. cup 4. plate
5. fridge 6. gloves 7. (spray) paint 8. judge
9. funeral

2. 1. herzlos 2. boshaft 3. angewidert 4. milde 5. lächerlich 6. verachtenswert

3. 1. Mr Albert Culper.
2. Last Thursday while he was at his wife's funeral.
3. Jewellery, a fur coat, a laptop computer, a television set and a video recorder.
4. They smashed furniture, ripped books apart, threw the contents of drawers and cupboards onto the floor and smeared everything with paint.
5. She had been invited to the funeral, but she hadn't been there. She was a drug addict. The police found clothes smeared with paint.
6. She, her mother and all the neighbours had helped her.
7. She thought the sentence was too lenient.
8. Individual solution

4. 1. The supermarket was broken into.
2. The building was ransacked.
3. Some spray cans were found.
4. Everything in the shop was destroyed.
5. A window was smashed.
6. The door was kicked in.
7. The man was rushed to hospital.
8. The number of the van was given to the police.
9. A hammer was used.

5. 1. arbeitslos 2. gedankenlos 3. endlos
4. zeitlos 5. unbezahlbar 6. obdachlos
7. leblos 8. hilflos 9. hoffnungslos

6. 1. daughter 2. funeral 3. one 4. addict
5. invited 6. accomplice 7. smashed 8. paint
9. bomb 10. hospital 11. clothes 12. name
13. prison

7. 1. (a glass of) beer 2. telephone box 3. motorbike 4. blanket
5. ambulance 6. wheelchair 7. van 8. shed

8. 1. together 2. coast 3. village 4. twice
5. pulse 6. injured

9. 1. Darts 2. emergency 3. hit-and-run 4. retirement
5. cousin 6. colleague

10. 1. F 2. T 3. F 4. T
5. F 6. F 7. F 8. T 9. F

Corrections:
1. The Mitchells were farmers and worked on their own farm.
3. Ralph Mitchell was tall and friendly.
5. P. C. Gregory Merton was the next person at the scene.
6. Gregory Merton got an e-mail.
7. The woman from New Zealand had once lived in Durham.
9. Mrs Merton didn't want her husband to find Terry Brewster.

Bildnachweis:

S. 16: Tür © Claude Huot, shutterstock.com, Nr. 163593326
Schlüssel: wikipedia.org
Fenster © InnaFelker, shutterstock.com, Nr. 175545527
Atemschutz © B. Wylezich, fotolia.com, Nr. 49585528
Teller © urfin, shutterstock.com, Nr. 124147882
Dose © Rainer Zenz, wikipedia.org
Flasche © Foto-Ruhrgebiet, fotolia.com, Nr. 30295730
Gorgonzolakäse © Gresei, fotolia.com, Nr. 49888158

S. 21: Fluss © Arseniy Krasnevsky, shutterstock.com, Nr. 147759620
Polizist © John Roman Images, shutterstock.com, Nr. 132200303
Führerschein © TrAj43, shutterstock.com, Nr. 47961076
Flasche © Foto-Ruhrgebiet, fotolia.com, Nr. 30295730
Brücke © Chris Jenner, shutterstock.com, Nr. 69083881
Menschenmenge © blvdone, shutterstock.com, Nr. 160644944

S. 24: Lippenstift: © Jen, wikipedia.org
Kapuzenpullover © Karkas, shutterstock.com, Nr. 39540556
Mantel © rustamir, fotolia.com, Nr. 40106129
Nagellack: wikipedia.org
Bluse © Karkas, shutterstock.com, Nr. 133206020
Rock © Karkas, shutterstock.com, Nr. 56346439
Jacke © Borislav Baijkic, shutterstock.com, Nr. 160400978
Mascara © wikipedia.org
Armbanduhr © Tarzhanova, shutterstock.com, Nr. 196227161
Einkaufstüte © stocksolutions, fotolia.com, Nr. 62068625

S. 34: Tor © Globalflyer, fotolia.com, Nr. 14291571
Brett © Harald Biebel, fotolia.com, Nr. 39302552
Mauer © Designers Fond Collection
Zaun © beermedia, fotolia.com, Nr. 44995802
Korb © monticello, shutterstock.com, Nr. 81546595
Würstchen © Frank C. Müller, wikipedia.org
Trillerpfeiffe © Thornard, wikipedia.org
Pokal © chones, fotolia.com, Nr. 60198888
Plastiktüte © MNI, shutterstock.com, Nr. 100130333

S. 38: Wohnwagen © PhotoWeges, shutterstock.com, Nr. 152200055
Fabrik © leungchopan, shutterstock.com, Nr. 179286233
Kellnerin © Sergey Nivens, shutterstock.com, Nr. 108274880
Dollar © Erwin Wodicka, fotolia.de, Nr. 31832998
Moped © Supertrooper, shutterstock.com, Nr. 148827953
Kunde © MEV
Motorrad © afxhome, fotolia.com, Nr. 35844770
Motorradhelm © Whyona, fotolia.com, Nr. 35523945
Motorradjacke © dresden, fotolia.com, Nr. 29550407
Kleiderschrank © Zerbor, shutterstock.com, Nr. 129368171
Damenmantel © rustamir, fotolia.com, Nr. 40106129
Stiefel © Olga Popova, shutterstock.com, Nr. 156736505
Schild "No smoking": wikipedia.org
Knie © westfotos.de, fotolia.com, Nr. 45232603
Bein © AXL, shutterstock.com, Nr. 163533059

Schöpfkelle © ILYA AKINSHIN, shutterstock.com, Nr. 182556146
US-Flagge: wikipedia.org
Britische Flagge: wikipedia.org

S. 52: Schmuck © rossella, shutterstock.com, Nr. 112070252
Pelzmantel © Monika3steps, shutterstock.com, Nr. 79548304
Tasse ©, shutterstock.com, Nr., 94467337
Teller © urfin, shutterstock.com, Nr. 124147882
Kühlschrank © Ljupco Smokovski, fotolia.com, Nr. 54582359
Handschuhe © Venus Angel, shutterstock.com, Nr. 127454756
Spraydose © elena agibalova, shutterstock.com, Nr. 97552133
Richter © bikeriderlondon, shutterstock.com, Nr. 122185735
Begräbnis © Kzenon, shutterstock.com, Nr. 143451874

S. 57: Bier © Nitr, shutterstock.com, Nr. 161089370
Telefonzelle © Martin Lisner, shutterstock.com, Nr. 159385130
Motorrad © afxhome, fotolia.com, Nr. 35844770
Decke © Visionär, fotolia.com, Nr. 38555226
Krankenwagen © KRoock74, wikipedia.org
Rollstuhl © SORG Rollstuhltechnik GmbH+Co.KG, wikipedia.org
Lieferwagen © Sven Storbeck, wikipedia.org
Schuppen © Shutterdo, shutterstock.com, Nr. 165127121